I0145543

Who am I to be Brilliant, Gorgeous, Talented and Famous?

Who am I to be Brilliant, Gorgeous, Talented and Famous?

By Dyanne Brown

© Copyright 2007 by M. Dyanne Brown
Printed in the United States of America

All rights reserved. No part of this publication may be reproduced, stored in a retrieval system, or transmitted in any form or by any means-electronic, mechanical, photocopy, recording, or any other-without the prior written permission of the publisher. The only exception is brief quotations in printed reviews.

Cover design: Marci Brown

Book layout: Marci Brown

ISBN: 978-0-6151-7819-6

I would like to dedicate this book to my family and friends. They continue to support me, put up with my ways and inspire me with their courage and power.

Introduction

The title of this book came from a quote by author and lecturer, Marianne Williamson. I heard the quote while watching a movie and it seemed as if the words passed through my spirit. I felt such a connection to the quote. In the quote, Marianne asks the question, "Who am I to be Brilliant, Gorgeous, Talented and Famous? Who am I not to be?" She goes on to explain that each of us is born with something that makes us special and we shouldn't diminish that and live small for the sake of others.

The poems in this book represent my journey to find my way back to my own light. I spent so many years hiding in the dark that I didn't even recognize my own light anymore. What I have learned in the process is that it hurts much more to fail on purpose than it does to fail by mistake. Being afraid to succeed is not honorable. You, not only let yourself down, but you let down the people around you that need you to be a shining example. Where would we be if our historic pioneers were living small? What if Dr. King never got involved with the Civil Rights movement or led the March? What if Harriet Tubman never traveled on the Underground Railroad? These heroes faced death to fulfill their purpose in life. No one knows if my purpose will be that great. The one thing I do know is that if I continue to live beneath my ability no one will ever find out.

I've wasted so much time and energy chasing material symbols of status. Happiness is not found in things-- it lies within. Now I understand that things are merely distractions from my true reason for being. In order to focus on my purpose, I have to block out all that noise and concentrate on my inner strength and God-given knowledge. In order to enjoy life, I can't allow the negativity to penetrate my core. I have to continue to laugh, feel brilliant, be gorgeous and if I'm lucky, I will be an example calling others to believe in themselves.

Table of Contents

Section 1: Learning to Love

Section 2: The Journey

Section 3: Reflections of A Stranger

Section 1:
Learning To Love

CHANGE IS THE ONLY CONSTANT

The only thing you can count on is change
what may be today
 won't be tomorrow
The puzzle may be clear at this moment; tomorrow it will be rearranged
and the picture will appear more clear
When I feel safe and comfortable
I know that an earthquake will come along and shake up my world
Break up the ground beneath my feet
Concrete shatters into bits
and I have to maintain my wits
Change is good
It's the only thing to trust
It's a rollercoaster
Just when you get used to the ride
It dips down
rides up high
does a loop to loop
and tosses you from side to side
You may close your eyes and you may even cry
but the excitement thrills you
It makes your blood race through your veins
Your heart pulses against your chest
tears pour from your eyes as you laugh until your stomach aches
Once you are safely on the ground
you will long for the time when you can ride again
Change is the dependable factor
It keeps life fresh
When you deny it, you wilt and spoil
Strap yourself in, throw your hands up and enjoy the ride
With change in your life, you never know what's waiting for you
around the next curve

VERVE PARASITES

Verve Parasites nosh on what's good in your life
while injecting you with their drama
They steal your happiness
leave you depressed and restless
if you let them
With microscopic views of their actions recognize their agenda
and slough them off before they attach
They are waiting for an opportunity
a vulnerability that allows them to get inside
Emotional vampires that suck your plasma
to sustain their own unhappy existence
When they bleed you dry, they will find a new host
unaware of their desire to destroy
that which seeks to help them thrive
Recognize verve parasites before they take your life
because they lack their own
They borrow from those that work hard
in order to find themselves a home
Never do they thank or show appreciation
because that would nourish your spirit
In order to keep you weak and defenseless
they withhold all love and affection
They dissect you piece by piece and
point out imperfections that are mere illusions
It's part of their collusion to keep confusion
at the forefront so you forget your own power
and they can continue to devour your greatness
When you feel uncomfortable and they wriggle in the night
It's time to put up a fight
Flush them out and set them free
so you can be the person you were meant to be

TWISTED ECLIPSE

I loved you at a time when I didn't even know what it meant to love myself
You became my focus
and we melded into one person, one personality
Your dreams became my aspirations
In you, I disappeared
I was lost and
I couldn't find myself because I didn't even know who I was
It wasn't your fault
The fault was mine, because I chose to hide
like the moon hides behind the sun
I was eclipsed and suffered in the darkness
Over time, I began to resent you
for not noticing that I was no longer here
I was mad at you for allowing me to fade away
You knew something was different, but couldn't quite figure it out
I was different
My love turned to rebellion
I fought against you, when in truth I allowed you to overshadow me
Emotionally, I blamed you for not fixing me
even though you didn't have the power
I twisted what was beautiful between us into something I could suffer
and before long you were gone
You moved on to find a less distorted love
In time, I found myself but it was too late for us
Painful memories have tarnished what could be
We can only remember what was
When I hid in your shadow
and we lost precious time while the darkness in my spirit
eclipsed the brightness of your shine

THE SINS OF THE FATHER

She suffers the sins of her father
for she will spend her life
trying to deny the familiarity that lives
behind her eyes
It's her punishment for being born to selfishness
and her penance for his bad decisions
She will spend her life searching for happiness
but subconsciously seeking to be miserable
Love comes with a price greater than she can comprehend
It's sickly twisted with pain and they lay incestuously in her mind
She will seek solace in the arms of a man that shares his likeness
and her soul will continue to suffer unrest
She will recreate his system of abuse
his distance and mistrust
because in her mind that is only way to love
In order to heal the wounds embedded deep in her heart
to smooth over the lacerations of disappointment
she must stitch them with jagged needles of misgivings
Only through her own pain will she find salvation
When she understands that her guilt lies not in her own lap
but in the sins of her father
Only then can she be washed clean and truly forgiven
and his debt will be fully repaid
She is whole once again

UNFINISHED

I denied myself the pleasure of your presence
until you demanded to be on my schedule
Like the fingers of a clock that caress the hours
you touch me in ways I've never felt before
reaching into my heart and massaging my soul
I can deny you no longer
Step inside my second and become a minute within my hour
and together we will control our time

SOMETHING'S MISSING

"Something's missing", she said
as she rested her hand on the place between her legs.
She didn't say it suggestively, but my eyes followed out of childlike curiosity.
She said it matter-of-factly and laughed when she heard me swallow hard.
"Chile, please", she waved my thoughts away
as she rested comfortably on the couch
I tried to find words to fill the silence, but she swallowed it whole.
"I've been missing it for so long that I can't remember what's gone.
You don't even hope for it anymore when it's been gone this long.
I used to be a lover of men, a player of sorts.
Women called me all types of sluts and whores,
but my relationship with each man was something special and dear to me.
It's not my problem that I had them in twos and threes."
She laughed and tossed her curls in the wind.
Her white teeth flashed as she hollered with reckless freedom.
She talked to me like I was her best friend.
"Men would call me Honey and buzz around me like bees.
Women buzzed as well, but they preferred to sting.
Never understood what their problem could be.
I didn't rest with husbands or anyone's man
I think they were just mad that I had the upper hand."
She pointed to her ample bosom and I understood
how a woman could feel inadequate against those two.
She lit a cigarette and took a deep drag.
Smoke rose through the air as she spoke again,
"Now, it's not like back then.
A man will climb all up in your stuff and still claim you're his friend.
He'll have women on the side and can't keep them in check.
You could lose your life after finding out about a girlfriend or wife.
Back then, it was more discreet.
There was more of an understanding between the women with men
that they knew roamed the streets.
Playboys weren't for marriage, but just for fun.
Now it seems like people will marry anyone."
The cigarette burned while nestled between her knuckles.
A string of ashes hung on the end before coming to rest in her lap.
She smiled at me and gave her knee a light slap.

"Something's missing", she said
as she rested her hand on the place between her legs.
"But I don't need it anymore.
When you learn how to live life and you learn how to love,
someone giving you their heart and trust is worth so much more.
That's what I have my husband for.
When you get to be my age, honey, then you will understand,
there is so much more when you find the right man."

THE BOTTOM OF THE BOTTLE

She found herself in the bottom of a bottle
Liquid therapy to kill the painful cancer of hurtful memories
that eat away at her soul
She finds the love she's never known
wrapped in a label of adulterated libations
Lowered inhibitions allow her to seek and conquer her temptations
taste the spicy sweet nectar of forbidden fruits
and in the morning suffer the consequences
She can't get back the lost moments of her youth
The thin veil between lucidity and incoherence flows through her mind
Some things she can remember and some are forever lost in time as
cells of memory die
and she remains blind to the price she pays every single day
Her trim figure is no more, no longer a face for a man to adore
Beautiful eyes hide behind drunken lids
A vibrant and full life replaced by barely wanting to live
Too many problems to survive and
hope has been killed too many times
She's faced so much disappointment and had love stomped on like grapes
that make the wine filling the glass
she brings to her lips to escape the pain
Half the time she feels like she's going insane
There's so much emotion bottled up that it spills over into her cup
Anguish lashes out in anger at the ones who love, but still hurt her
Blind eyes see what they want to see
Her cries for help are ignored, because it would require too much of them
It's easier to let her suicide in the darkness of herself
then for someone to extend a hand
She takes all the blame
Killing her gradually with each sip
Locked in a vicious cycle that plays out each night
Pain, think, drink, pain, think, drink
until she's numb and still
Nothing left to think and nothing left to feel
They found her in the bottom of a bottle
and even though it doesn't seem right
It was the first time in a long time that she had a peaceful night
Now they wish they had done something
to try and save her life

SACRIFICES

I constantly find myself
giving up something important to me
Rearranging my day
to fit into the time table of another
Altering my plans
to support a friend or lover
Those who are nowhere to be found
when I'm struggling to keep my head above water
But I don't blame them
It's my choice to give them the power
When they beckon, I come running
Pretending that I'm okay with it
That my plans didn't matter
When deep inside I'm seething
at once again being denied
the appreciation I so strongly desire
Beneath the surface, it burns like fire
Anger boils my blood
Once again I am there for someone
that, in turn, I would never count on.
doing things that I don't really want to
Just so that I can maintain my martyr status
I denounce their ability to be as great a friend as me
because they could never give as much as I have
In truth, there is no barter system in friendship
They shouldn't have to repay my kindness
if I'm truly sacrificing for the right reasons
You don't give in order to get in return
You give from the heart purely for the joy of it being received
My friends and family have been deceived
The biggest fool of all was me
For I believed, that love had to cost me everything
when the price is actually genuine
Giving out of insecurity desires a spotlight
It requires to be rewarded through artificial means
Giving from the heart does not require replenishment
For the heart delights in the act of kindness and receives its rewards in
knowing it is appreciated without ever hearing it
The lesson I learned is that when you give more than you can afford
You sacrifice the greatest thing you can own
Love for yourself

BORN OF THIS WORLD

We are born into a world of violence
in a violent way
Pushed from our warm surrounding
then yanked from our home and sense of security
Once muffled voices are now filled with vibrato
A smack delivers the eagerly awaited cry that proves life
Proves that we recognize pain and discomfort
Our parents prepare us for life in this world
and all its dangers
They subject us to small hurts so that we can sidestep larger pains
in the future when we are on our own
However, there is a part of us that never believes in those unforeseen dangers
For good reason, because we wouldn't explore life
if we swallowed whole our parent's neurosis
We are designed to explore the world and hopefully make it better
We are pieces of our parents but wholes of ourselves
We can't find out who we are by replicating their lives
We must develop our own terms
We must make and learn from our own mistakes
We must fall and rise and sometimes fall again only to rise again
and then one day we will have our own child
and we will make our own mistakes
The cycle continues

LEARNING TO LOVE

She was just a girl
a girl who felt unloved, unappreciated, and unseen
a girl lost in the eyes of others
a girl with budding hips and sexuality on her lips
that she was unaware of

In words from men, she found the attention
she so sorely missed
In the eyes of men, she saw the love
that she had always wished
on a shooting star from the sky
she chased the feeling and believed the lie
that ultimately killed the little girl inside

She gave to fill their need
she didn't understand the deed
but if that was what it took to see what she saw in their eyes
she didn't have to ask why

She wanted to feel love
she wanted to feel loved
she wanted to feel it deep down inside
where she felt empty
where the little girl learned to hide

As hard as she tried
They never could fill the hole
she still felt hollow and unworthy
she still felt ugly and dirty
and in her long life she never knew
that the power that she needed
what she seeks rest deep inside
her own heart

She was the one who loved and treated her right
but it was not enough
and her life ended on concrete streets
lifeless left in a dream of Love
joining to validate her life

I'M NO BITCH

I do not give you the right to call me out of my name
I was born as someone special, a child of God,
so why would I answer to anything else?

I do not give you permission to degrade me in any way
I am blessed with the challenge of giving birth
I am a giver of life and part of the earth
You cannot diminish my greatness in an effort to make yourself look greater

I do not allow you to make me any less than I am
I am the partner to man
I was given life to be a companion
I am the nurturer
The sun and the rain, mother of nature
You cannot deny me my crown
by trying to put me down

I will not now, nor will I ever
be the image in music videos or in songs
I'm no bitch or hoe
I'm none of the words used to steal my power
I am every second, minute and hour of every day in every year
I am your mother, your sister, your grandmother
Your aunt and your daughter
I am your wife and your partner
I am a woman
I am a gift to man, children and the earth
I will not now, nor will I ever give credence
or condone the explanation
to the degradation
of me

I LIVE

I'm walking through life like a zombie
Numb to feeling and never really seeing things the way they are
Just drifting, coasting along, doing my day-to-day
Allowing life to live me, instead of living life
Never seeing beyond the boundaries of a city block

I'm a love Frankenstein fastened together by broken hearts.
cancerous lies and lost dreams
Tell me what, what would I do if I could feel
and to know that what I'm feeling is for real?
Maybe genuine tears would fall from my eyes
and release the pain that I suppress deep inside

The only thing that wakes me from my slumber
is not a magical kiss from a Prince
or some magic fairy dust as in every childhood tale
The black cloak of death shocks me from my blindness
Death lay at my feet and I see that my tomorrow is not promised
He takes my loved ones, one by one,
jolting me into action to avoid their pitfalls to preserve my own existence
I know now that life is for living

It took knowing death to make me choose life
Sleeping with death like an intimate lover,
feeling him invade my world
and steal my gifts
Leaving my naked heart exposed and vulnerable
My time has not come
I climb from the darkness of Hades
into the sunlight and feel the rebirth of my soul
I live

i hate u

i hate u
i'll say it 10 times fast
and a 100 times slow
the best thing I ever did for me was to let you go
i wish i could've let you know
just how much
i hate u
you toyed with my feelings
and played with my heart
you fed me words of love
and like a starving child
i ate heartily of them and didn't worry if actions were to follow
you left my heart hollow
you burrowed in like a leach and sucked my soul dry
you drank in the tears that i cried
when you stared in my eyes and lied
i waited around patiently
like an addict
until you decided i deserved another hit
and i paid heavily for your love with my self-esteem
you were my drug
tearing me apart on the inside
just for a minute of a love high
floating on a cloud
feeling like someone in this world cares about me
when really you could care less
i might have been waiting to exhale
but you made me lose my breath
when you smothered me with your hatred
you are the worst evil that exists
you act like you love when really you just want to break women down
once they fall in love, then you are never around
you kill their spirit and swallow them whole
you inspire doubt
you break trust
you force them into despair
until they are so starved for affection
they will do anything to hold on to what they think is love
you are the devil in disguise
i hate you so much right now
that it runs from my toes to my head from my nerves through my veins

it pumps through my heart and feeds my mind
maybe it will go away with time
but for right now it should certainly explain
i hate you so much that I can't speak your name
i'll call you evil, simple and pure
i should've never invited you in my life
i felt the cold when you came through my door
darkness fills your heart and spills from your lips
i fooled myself into believing that I could change you
good would conquer all
instead, you made me hateful
the truth is that what I hate about you is the same thing I hate about me.
i guess I should be grateful
because without the pain from you I would never see
this ugliness that I hate inside of me

CHANGE IS GONNA COME

I lay it down
I lay it down before thee
I accept the transformation
You have planned for me
I'm not fighting anymore
I finally believe that I do deserve more
I silence the noise that fills my ears
I face my fears
I'm not afraid of change any longer
Dissolve my tears
I lay it down before thee
I give myself to you
Change me for the better
I'm ready to live a new way for the rest of forever
No longer running away
Putting on my new face at the start of every day
Looking at everything through new eyes
Less of a know-it-all and more open to "why"
I lay it down
I lay it down before thee
The one that I thought I had to be
I give myself to you
Submit to your perfect will

CINDERELLA

I thought the shoe fit
when I slid it on my foot but
I was wrong
You were not the Prince Charming that I thought would rescue me
but I love you anyway
I had it all wrong
Love is not fairytale perfect
It's not something that just happens
It's engineered and put in motion and
it's up to the conductors to keep it on track
A relationship requires upkeep and service
It has to be believed in, desired, nurtured,
nourished, grown and, at times, pruned
It's not about being rescued
You have to save yourself
You can't place your fate in the hands of someone else
I recognize that it's my responsibility to make love what it is
I can't leave it to someone else to make me happy
There is no happily ever after
If the happy times outweigh the sad times
then the relationship is right
With this new knowledge of love, I kicked off the glass slipper
and put it away
We'll save the fantasy for someone else
reality will do us just fine

INSPIRATION

I'm inspired by you
Few things in this world have
the power to move me like you do
I am in awe of who you chose to be
I am saluted by your presence
I am strengthened by not only the beauty of your spirit
but your soul and your essence
I find you simply amazing
and feel lucky to watch you in motion
The love in your heart is like a potion
rendering me helpless to my own insecurities
I can do nothing but to love you
I couldn't resist even if I tried
You see not only the me that I present to the world,
but the me that lives inside
You look beyond my eyes to the dark pieces that I try to hide
into my very soul
You sympathize and empathize
You anesthetize and emphasize
You surprise and realize
You've not only shown me that I have wings
but always believed I would fly
Everything I am
Everything I will be
Everything I hope for
Everything I do
will now and always be inspired by you

SUNSHINE

It rises to illuminate the darkness of night
Ushering in the dawn
Moving slowly across the ground
Chasing shadows away
and sending the flowers into yawn
Nourishing the birds and bees
Rooster's crow and alarms howl
as morning has arrived
Feet swung over the bed crash to the floor
Stumble blindly to the bathroom
Rushing to get dressed and out the door
Coffee brews and muffins rise
as bodies move about in a rush
to fill vacant office chairs
The day moves quickly as the sun
moves across the sky
High noon welcomes the lunch rush
Appetites carry tired minds and
drained bodies to seek nourishment
They are renewed in the sun
Life energy is restored
They work some more
Tired sun greets eager moon
as exhausted bodies make their way home
and others come to life
we rest our eyes for sleep and dream
until the next sun rise

DAYS GONE BY

I think about him sometimes
He that I once called love
He that I continued to measure love by long after he was gone
No one could compare to the love that he gave me
even though he never gave me much
In my mind, he was everything at the time
He was love to me back when I knew nothing about being in love
When I was naïve, painting love as something you see on TV
compared to my narrow view
He was everything a girl could want
loyal in the hours that we spent together
I never questioned the hours spent apart
until he taught me to be suspicious by feeding me lies
I thought he was so wise
He told me about life and how I should live it
He told me about my money and how I should spend it
He became all encompassing; my world
He was everything I needed when I didn't know I had needs
He was safety when I didn't recognize my own shields
As I grew older we drifted apart
From time-to-time I think of him
He that taught me what love is not
I loved him when I thought love had to hurt to be real
I loved him when I didn't have the ability to feel
I loved him when I was afraid of love and all its responsibilities
I love him when I hated me
I think about him sometimes
He wasn't a bad guy
He showed up at the wrong time
He was the catalyst to my progression
He never had my total affections
He was there to make me understand
that love was so much more than I knew
For that, I thank him
He was the victim of my desire to learn and grow
and he will never truly know
how much I loved him
I think about him sometimes
when the sun kisses the moon as it descends for its daily slumber
We were two hearts passing in the night
and I remember him in days gone by

BAD BLOOD

I wish I could have felt it coursing through my veins
burning my future and changing my name
I thought he was bringing me love
he brought death to my door
etched my name in stone
with a date soon to be determined
much earlier than once believed
I thought he was bringing me happiness
he gave me a lifetime of fear
wondering which breath will be my last
sickens me to my stomach
resting in my throat
like the pills that preserve my health
dissolving into yesterdays
I thought he was giving me a chance
that's gone now
I'll never know the child that I can't bare
my hopes are buried like
the tracks of the needles in his arms
he didn't care to show
his medical news
afraid to lose someone I never really had
an illusion of something I'll never see
forever is no longer an option
It was stolen from me
I thought he was giving me my dream
I wish I could've felt it before
I allowed him to fill me up with lies
I am in this room
Hooked up to IV's and melodic machines
Monitoring my every breath and heart beat
Feeding me life through a tube
thinking back to what I could've changed
if I cared more about me
you see what he gave me
was a lesson learned
H I V
through my blood
I was burned
now it's taken what I gave away
MY LIFE

NO WONDER

If I ever wondered what love is
Love is personified in your eyes
It is the destiny that guided us to be at the same space in time
It is the obstacles I faced that refined me until I became the mold
that would perfectly join with you
It is the place that was carved inside your heart for me to live
It is times when I love you so passionately that it hard to control

If you ever wondered if it's true
Don't listen to my words because my actions will reflect
The smile that shapes my lips when you are by my side
I rearrange and bend time to be in your presence
I pray at night for your health and welfare
When you cry even the sunniest day appears grey
I'll worry for you, let me take your fears away

If you've ever wondered how this could be
It is because of who you are
You are love as love should be
You are the perfect one for me
You are God's gift to the days in my life
You fill the space that was surely designed especially for you
Believe that you deserve to be loved the way I want to love you

If you've ever wondered how long this can last
Forever is not long enough
I will love you through time
If I leave you too soon, I'll come back for you
to make sure you always feel loved
I pledge my heart and my devotion
through each continent and across the ocean
My soul will connect and try to find you

If you've ever wondered, wonder no more
Love is standing here
Love is yours

DAMAGED GOODS

Heart for sale
to the highest bidder
and if you buy it
I don't know if you are the winner
this heart is damaged
from years of abuse
I hope you can repair it
and put it to good use
it's never been loved
or cared for right
It's never been protected
or held tight at night
It's sadly neglected
and full of mistrust
This heart won't believe a word you say
This heart will question why you stay
This heart will try to push you away
It's damaged beyond repair
It's no damn good
Just to be fair
and make sure I'm understood
This heart will not love without question
This heart will not show you true affection
This heart is surrounded by its own protection
Do you still want it?
Are you sure you want to buy?
Do you want to give a heart like this a try?
To the highest bidder, it is sold
 Hopefully, you can turn this poor old heart into gold

FORGIVENESS

I've been locked in this pain so long that I don't know how to be without it
I don't know who I am without anger and hurt to fuel my actions
At times, I worry that it will sap my strength to let down my shield
and allow myself to love when there is the fear of vulnerability
Allowing someone else the opportunity to know me
also gives them the chance to hurt me
and I would only have myself to blame
I could no longer blame you for everything that goes wrong
I can't use you as an excuse
I can't imagine life without the stress
and the exhausting haunting of past transgressions
What will I think about when I am not replaying past events in my mind?
How will I spend all this newfound free time?
If I forgive you, how can I exact my revenge for things that
you probably no longer remember?
How can I continue to complain and gain sympathy about my tough life?
If I forgive, it would require me to actually live and that frightens me
I'm comfortable locked in this prison of anguish
watching the muscles of my future atrophy
feeling my prospects wither away as I starve for affection
Hate invading the veins like a dangerous infection
stealing my health and leaving me thirsty for attention
To step outside the bars would require something great of me
To give you my forgiveness would relieve my suffering and misery
and set myself free from this self-inflicted torture.
I guess I'll just wait for my parole to decide
The decision comes from me
For the warden, judge and jury exist inside
From justice, there is nowhere to hide
I guess Forgiveness is what it will have to be
and the sentence is life

DAY OF EBONY

She carries sorrow in her heart
but she chooses not to show it
She must press on for those that will never appreciate her effort
Love is lost on her, because she'll never know it
She can't recognize it any longer
because she's given too much
She passed her threshold and now she can't accept much more
A smile will dance across her lips when she'd really like to cry
Anger will erupt from her mouth to hide her feelings inside
She's been hurting for so long and doesn't even recognize it
because she's too busy trying to bury it beneath an earth of lies
and she doesn't even realize
that she wears them within the darkness of her eyes
Happiness is no longer hers to embrace
Sadness is what she must face
If she wants to find her way back, she's gone too far
She's given too much
She has nothing left for anyone else
not even herself
which is truly a shame because her personality is electric
Enough to light an entire city block for seven hundred days
When she digs deep and finds herself it will be a triumph
She's been lost for so long
that she doesn't even know the person she could be
One day I know that she will see what I see
She is like the sun on a hot summer day
It's unapologetic for its intensity, but comforting in its tenacity
It warms not only the day, but leaves more for the night
It works hard to make everything alright
It's giving to a fault
and only when it understand its limits
when it knows what it means to the world
is when she'll truly know that she is appreciated and loved
is when she embraces forgiveness

THE DANCERS

Music moves her feet across the floor
She glides, sways and through the air soars
Her heart directs the emotions into her limbs
Legs rising to the sky
Toes pointed and muscles flexing
Her arms follow invisible notes
Floating through the room
and reaching out to heaven

She joins with her partner
Lifting her to heights and supporting her weight
He moves in compliment of her style
They come together to interpret the music
They separate and rejoin
They fly, she slides and he twirls her
as partners they work together

He peers deep into her eyes
and she is reassured that he will always be there to catch her
She feels safe in his arms, as she continues to dance,
to express her feelings through her moves
The wind urges them to push harder
They dance with all their energy and vigor
until the song ends and they can dance no more

Section 2:
The Journey

THE JOURNEY

You explored regions that you were not allowed
Traveling with no permission and against your better judgment
to undiscovered and untouched territory
Creating awareness before its natural progression
Invading its perfection and turning something beautiful
into something ugly for your own sick satisfaction

Eden was desecrated and destroyed by greed
Mentally raped and left to believe
that is was of my own desire and need
When in truth, I was too naïve
to understand or agree

You violated my life before I had a chance to be me
Changed me into someone with no control
an illusion of strength and vitality
In actuality a victim struggling with daily life
Trust never thriving in my garden
Hope barely surviving among the weeds of despair
you planted in the soil of my dreams

So I spend my days giving myself away
Selling my soul in pieces to strangers
Living in fear that they would steal it like you
if I didn't offer it first
In order to circumvent the pain, I gave it on my own terms
Faulty beliefs beget salacious results
The delusion of protection was another dagger
in the wound created by you

There is still a chance to live
To remove this wall of pain that I've built
The work is arduous and the agony is palpable
Digging will unearth ugly truths and realizations
but it must be done to restore the beauty that once was
It's required in order to find deserved love
With bloody knuckles and tear-streaked cheeks,
I stitch the wound with threads of modified beliefs
What was done to me was not meant to be my end
but to be the fuel for the journey of my new beginning.

THIS OLD HEART OF MINE

Open my heart
It's been closed for so long
that for awhile I thought it wasn't possible
Then you came along
and changed everything
You raised the stakes and took a real risk
This old heart of mine
been hurt for so many years
that it's built up a wall of fears
to keep outsiders from getting inside
You walked right in as if the wall didn't exist
You found a space and made yourself a home
as if you'd never known
You must have noticed my apprehension
at the mere mention of loving you back
but you didn't seem to care
It was almost as if it was a dare
It made you work that much harder to win me over
Within this heart you planted roses
and nurtured them to bloom
I didn't think anything could live inside my heart
much less grow and thrive
Seeing that made me realize that I'm alive
Through your love I see life in a different way
I look forward to each new day
I must admit that I'm completely surprised
I can't go back to the way things used to be
Now I'm used to having you here with me
I knew that things would be different when we met
but I never could've known or bet
that you could've opened my heart
the way that you've done
That's why you are the one
that forever changed my life
by healing this old heart of mine

THIS MUCH I KNOW

She laughed and a wrinkle formed in the corner of her eye
She said, "Chile, I can only tell you what I've learned so far
and I have so far to go. See me in a couple years and I tell you again.
This much I know.

Love doesn't come with a price.
If it does, then you should think twice.
It shouldn't cost your self-respect or your pride;
the only way you pay is in attention and time.
If it's right, you will give those willingly
and that's how love should be.
It can be a struggle and some compromise,
but you should never have to give up your total being
just to be in a relationship
Love should nurture you and make you feel strong.
If it steals your strength, then something's wrong.

Life is designed for your edification.
Everything around you is apart of the lesson
intended to help you grow into the person you are supposed to be.
If you open up your eyes and see
you won't missing the blessings being bestowed.
It's to help you drop the baggage that you carry in tow,
so you live the life that you can be proud of.
Now, back to love
You can spend your entire life trying to sort out childhood pain.
Pausing your life while waiting for someone to explain
something that doesn't require an explanation.
People are people and it's a fact.
Your parents were people before and after they were parents.
They tried to be perfect for you, but that was never possible.
You are an individual with your own thoughts and needs.
Stop blaming them for not knowing what they couldn't know.
It's like blaming the rain for causing the weeds.
Everything grows at the same rate and with the same nourishment.
Parents provide the seed and the feed, but you are responsible for the
outcome.
You chose what you will be."

She laughed and a sparkle twinkled in her eye
She continued to speak,

"Let me tell you about material things.
Everyone wants to have the biggest, hottest and newest thing.
Trying to top your neighbor or friend with the latest trend.
Spending money that you don't have just to look special
when it's really not required.
Putting yourself in debt when it's never necessary.
Why owe someone else just to impress another?
Material things are just things and mean nothing to your spiritual growth.
They are mere distractions from the life you deserve.
They dig you deeper into a ditch that you can't get out of
trying to obtain these material trappings.
While you wallow in debt,
your neighbor doesn't even know or care that you tried to impress them
nor do they know how much money you've spent.
All to look like you have more than you actually do
and the stress is suffered only by you.
Heartaches and attacks ensue.

If only people focused on the things that matter:
Spending time with children and developing a life.
Divorce would decrease and cease to exist.
Adore your children and love your wife.
Stop worshipping material wealth.
Pay more attention to your health.
Lead the revolution
since the beginning of evolution, we've looked to you
and you've let us down.
It's time to pick your crown.
Our children need you.
Our women need you.
Our men need you.
We all need you.
It's time for a brand new leader.
It's time for a brand new speaker.
It's time.
This much I know, so where are you?"

THE MASK

I chose not to wear the mask that was created for me
The mask that everyone wants to see
What lies beneath this beautiful facade is even more natural beauty
to the eye of the fortunate beholder
The beauty will only cultivate as I grow older
It's the wisdom in my eyes that he'll desire
The sharpness of my mind that will stroke his fire
and my heart that will take him higher and higher
Laughing makes the body ache, but never tire
He will see me as I am, was and always will be
The mask I won't hide behind
I offer the real me

THE GIFT

If I could be lost in you for a few hours
It would make the other twenty-one fly by
If I could bathe in your affection
All reality would feel like a subtle lie
I would know the truth
while others wish for fantasy
When I bask in all that is you
Your words flow through me like Nile water
in my past history
Your touch is like an oasis in the middle of the Serengeti
You quench my thirst
and arouse my hunger
in one breath
I'm imprisoned by the loneliness of existence
waiting patiently for you to emancipate
the woman I could be
As the earth revolves
Day turns into night
Dusk til Dawn
Midnight to morning light
I look to the heavens and thank God for this heavenly gift
that rests on the pillow next to me
in the disguise of the man
that has the eyes that recognize
the true beauty that lies inside

FIGHT

It always starts slowly with words
Normal everyday words
The kind exchanged with no real thought
Used to rattle off the grocery lists and describe workdays
To gossip about family and friends
Abruptly it changes like thunder in the middle of a hot summer day
Calm voices escalate into shouts until they boil into full-blown yelling
Accusations and curses fly about the room
bouncing off the walls like daggers sailing towards their target
They cut deep creating wounds and injuries
 that are barely noticed as the battle ensues
Faces nose-to-nose locked in intimidating stances
Hours from tranquility, but seconds from fisticuffs
The fighters are not the same height, same weight or even the same sex
We shouldn't be in this fight
Large hands push against my chest and send me crashing into the wall
Smashing picture frames of the children we love
Exploding and shattering into pieces as they hit the floor
A moment of clarity tells me that I don't want to fight
We've gone too far and I've been through this many times before
I make an effort to get to the phone
Foolishly believing that this time I will make it
knowing that this beast is poised to halt my advance
My cheek explodes in searing pain
While I'm still reeling, I can feel his fingers digging into my throat
My feet are no longer touching the floor.
He continues to shout as my mouth starts to bleed
I can taste the familiar salty liquid between my teeth
This is the third time this week
My mind is racing trying to figure out what got me here
and how to get out of it
What's the right thing to say and what could I have done wrong
My throat is free as I fall to my feet and crumble to the floor
I roll into a ball as he pummels my body with fists of steel
I pray for relief and an opportunity to retreat
Once he feels that I have learned his desired lesson
When he gets tired I know the threat will lessen
One would wonder why I endure such abuse
Because when the times are good, they are the best
Where would I go?

The excuses I tell myself
as I nurse the bumps and bruises
He's not a bad guy he just has a bad temper
I know someday things will get better
when I learn how to not make him mad
It's really not that bad
At least he apologizes every time
Mama says that one day he'll kill me
That's something that I try not to think of
For now we'll just try to work it out
These are the types of things on my mind
as my body accepts the punishment for this type of love
The storm begins to subside
He finally leaves the room
I pick myself up and survey the damage
Minor cuts and bruises
Broken glasses and groceries strewn
This is our life
This is the way we love
We survive fight-to-fight
We get along from night-to-night
Don't worry about me, because I'll be alright
I can handle the pain
I've been doing it all my life

ROMANTIC ROAD

Rose petals on the floor from the door to the bedroom
The bathroom lit by candlelight with a bath drawn for two
Dinner waiting in the kitchen and
all I have to do is arrive for a night of romance
It's not as much the act as it is the planning
that touches my heart and lets me know how much you value me
In planning you thought of what I would like
and there was a great deal of thought and time
poured into this act
It makes my heart overflow
Erasing any question as it shows
just how much you appreciate all that I do
Whisk me away for a day together
doing things we love to share
There's no expense to spare
and this is one night when I don't have to feel like
a mother or a wife
I just feel treasured and adored
We talk for hours, but not about normal things
Instead of daily tasks or bills and money
We discuss our hopes and dreams and the things that make us happy
I feel hopeful again and love renewed
as my heart is revived by the attention from you
Sometimes we move through life with our blinders on
We expect to receive what we are fortunate to have
and we forget to thank the person providing the experience
It only takes a moment to remember what it is about them you love
to take them back to the way your love began
Receive in love and reward the same way
Don't forget to create a special day
Happiness is not a destination
It is the journey itself
It takes work to stay on the right path
Romance is a road on the path that you will pass many times
The choice to stop and visit is your own
but it's necessary if you don't want to take the journey alone

RATING

Hmm...let's see
How exactly would I rate me?
Surprisingly that's hard question
that requires a bit of digestion
I rarely ever focus on me
long enough to think about it
but since I've been asked
let me try to commit
Well I've survived a lot
Most that I don't care to share
but that could've have broken my spirit
and left me deep in despair
but I picked myself up, broken pieces and all
held my head high and stood tall
I've accomplished some things
that others refused to believe
They told me I couldn't do it
They told me I wouldn't succeed
They expected me to come back
begging on my knees
telling them I was wrong and they were right
but they didn't know that I can fight
I don't just take what's handed
I go after the prize
I got knocked down and they watched me rise
Time after time
Sure I could use a nip here and tuck there
I could learn more
I could be more
I could change my hair
I could be someone's wife or someone's mother
I could be someone's special lover
I could be one thing or another
but this moment
this minute
this very hour
If you ask me to rate myself, I'll count my power
My strength is a ten and so is my spirit
My voice is a ten, cause you are sure to hear it
My heart is a ten and filled with love
My mind is a ten because I know how to use it

50

What makes my body a ten is that no one can abuse it
My soul is a ten cause it draws you to it
My laughter's a ten cause you can't refuse it
My talent's a ten cause it's God given
My life is a ten cause of the way I'm livin
My past is a ten because it's all forgiven
It all adds up to what I'm a percentage of
I'm 110% of God's Love.

LADY DAY

Her song rose from the depths of her soul
                     and flowed from her lips like a caged bird
It soared through the room with the rawness of deep suffering
Recognition filled listening ears
                      inspiring relation and spilling tears
Vacancy in her eyes
           Death in her midst
                She used poison to take the anguish away
It coursed through her veins robbing her talent
                            and stealing her youth
Darkness hiding one half of her frame
White rose in her hair shining in the spotlight
Silver microphone kissed by crimson lips
Hands caress the stand that rests on the wooden stage
          God Bless the Child
                but forgotten she felt
                     as her relief was denied time after time
Flawless notes floated through the air
                joined with exquisite agony
                      to produce a tale to tell
Beauty remembered in the memories of pictures
             as her rose withered in time
                 as the world continues to turn
History remembers
         the child that's got its own
            that's got its own

GOD IS LOVE

There's this immaculate love that exists inside me
When I go inside my mind, He rests within immense calm
It's like the silence that falls on a city when it snows
Omniscient, but always absorbing the surroundings
Ever expounding

This tiny voice that distinguishes right from wrong
speaks softly but loudly disagrees
He doesn't admonish wrongdoing
He reminds that I have the freedom of choosing
but quietly hopes for compliance
even in the face of clear defiance

He seeks to prepare me even when I can't see
through trials and obstacles
Reminds me of His omnipotent presence
through seemingly impossible connections
He speaks through others' actions
and uses their words to provide me knowledge
He teaches through loss and rewards with gains

He never gives up and continues to support
When I fall, He helps me to my feet
When I'm weak, He carries me
When I hurt, He heals my bruises
When I'm lost, He reveals the truth
Ever present and always aware
He's always there
Inside my heart

I REALIZE

I realize
that I like the way I see myself
in your eyes
I've never known this before
What a surprise
I'm used to diverted stares
to disguise
The guilt of words
Full of lies
in the past I devised
a plan that would expose you
it never came to be
so now I surmise
that your love is in fact true

CONFESSIONS OF A PLAYER

Despite popular misconception
Players are not conceived
They are born of regular means
Somewhere in their life they suffer from being deceived
At that point, they decide that they will spend their lives
avoiding the same type of pain
that family member, lover or friend administered
by hardening their heart for further protection
The deceived becomes the deceiver and they seek out believers
The cycle continues and loneliness infects yet another
The Player is in denial of his or her own damaged mentality
leading to the inability to understand the pain they create
Each lover is paying the price
and is merely a casualty
in the war the player has waged against the original deceiver
Unhappiness is all they find
as the money and getting over doesn't bring them joy
Never does it heal the wound created
All it succeeds in doing is pulling them further and deeper
into the pain they expected to avoid and makes
the player feel more unlovable as lovers become wise to the hurtful actions
They find only frustration and no satisfaction
Ultimately, they pay the price of following the same path
In the end, the player gets played
for when he or she is laid to rest
no one sheds tears of true unconditional love
Only tears for what could've been

IN LOVE
(for John and Kazina McGettigan)

There was a time when I had given up on love
I decided that it was too hard and I was better off without it.
Love pursued me in a way that I've never known.
Love wouldn't give up until I recognized it.
It appeared in a way that I wasn't used to.
I resisted.
I had this picture in my mind of how it would be;
this fantasy of a knight in shining armor,
but love was not loud and shiny
Love snuck in quietly.
It crept into my life in such a way that I couldn't shield myself.
My heart opened up and let love in before I even knew.
I found myself feeling things that I never knew I could feel
and from the lips of love came words that proved to me
that is was indeed real.
It tore my emotional walls to the ground then built them up around us.
It's my security and warms me when nights are cold.
When I doubt myself, love takes my hand and reminds me
that I no longer stand alone.
It loves me even when I'm not sure I can love myself.
When I feel at my worst, love sees my beauty.
It's here when I feel like I have nobody else.
Love forgives me even when I know I'm wrong.
Love compromises just so that we can get along.
It feeds me when I'm starving for affection.
Love has surpassed my every expectation;
it requires little to no explanation.
When I think of the saying that love is blind
I now know that we are blind to some of the finer details that love brings;
the small sacrifices that are hidden behind a grand gesture.
Love is standing before me and offering me forever
and when I see love, it's in your reflection
and in your reflection
I see myself
in love.

GIVE YOUR HEART TO ME

Give your heart to me
whether we agree or disagree
If we have a big fight and sleep on separate sides of the bed for a night
in the morning, let me know my place in your heart is all right
Love me through the lows and highs
Happiness and sadness
The when, where's and why's
Love me more when you understand me less
Love me at my worst and my best
Love me even if I digress

Allow me to give my heart to you
in the moment when you feel the weakest, I'll be strong
I'll love you when you're right and wrong
even in the times when we don't get along
I'll stand behind you and support your stance
I'll appreciate our deeper love and true romance
Join me
Take my hand and share eternity
Pledge with complete sincerity
Give your heart to me
Allow me to give my heart to you
and love will always see us through
til the end of all time

WASH OVER ME

The thoughts you gather when thinking of me
are cleansed of all insecurities and societal influences
You see me as I am
and in your eyes I see myself as I want to be
I am in awe of your unique approach to the world
and appreciative that you allow your essence
to spill through words of wisdom
into my thoughts and actions
You are not selfish or afraid to share your years
of gathered knowledge and lessons
You allow me to sip when I am thirsty and
eat voraciously when I am starving
but you tap my wrists ever so graciously
when I forget to mind my manners
I grew up without the delicate balance of patience and aggressive furor
I was not taught the rules of engagement
You humbly remind me that life
is not always about the battle but how we endure
It's not always about what we have but what it is for
God always has something in store
and it's so much more
than I could ever conceive on my own
You teach me
you guide me
you deny and oblige me
You allow your love to wash over me
as a river washes over a rock
in constant motion and with such force
until that rock has no choice, but to yield to the river
Over time, what was once rough becomes smooth and polished
A thing of beauty
a fossil of life
an imprint in the earth
and apart of the world that surrounds it
When the river has receded and the rock stands on its own
it gleams in the sun like the jewel it was created to be
priceless

YOU LIED

I can no longer pretend
that I don't know what you've been up to
I can't close my eyes any longer
and wish it away
I can't deny that I love you just a little less
and hate you just a little more with each passing day
Every morning you look into my eyes
and lie to my face
telling me where you say you will be
when I know in my heart that you'll be at her place
It kills me inside to know that
I pretend that you successfully hide your trespasses
when friendly spies apprise me of your whereabouts
I could fool myself, but I can't fool the eyes of others
Trying to hold this illusion of togetherness up to the world
It was slowly crumbling in my own mind
Suffering and dying over time, because you lied
You're snipes of disrespectful conduct
have assassinated my hopes for the future
murdered my sense of trust
and desecrated our love
I'm slowly putting myself back together
like pieces of a puzzle
One piece will forever be missing
The piece of my heart that departed with your lies

SOBER

Each days is a struggle
Stress tempts me to the bottle
but my mind reminds that I can handle it
The liquor calls my name
Some days it taunts me
that I will no longer feel that familiar burn
or the numbness it provides
Each event is a hurdle
Watching others imbibe
without a thought of trouble
almost tricks my mind
into believing that I'm strong enough to
Then I'm reminded of flashes of the costs of that liquid treat
I chose to resign myself to alternative comforts
Each night is a triumph
I have won the battle, but not yet the war
Day-by-day is how I take it

CRAZY THOUGHTS

For so long, I thought I was the one with all the answers
It turns out that I'm really the one with all the questions
Each one of them lying deep inside hidden beneath
A lifetime of unspoken confessions
These secrets plague me like tiny viruses within my body
Breaking me down emotionally
but keeping me alive to feel the torture
of the sting they create inside
and the weakness it shows outside
My appearance screams that I'm out of control
I wear the mask everyday that I've got it all together
when honestly I could fall apart
I'm all over the place in my mind
Tied together by strings that could easily break
I thought the best thing for everyone was to never tell
To never speak of the horror that sometimes seems like a dream
More like a nightmare
Every time I wake I wonder if I was really there
but then I rationalize, if I wasn't why would I dream it
Minds don't conjure up those types of dreams
out of nowhere
My subconscious is begging me to breathe
It's begging me for health
trying to get me to save myself
but I can't
It would mean that I'd have to admit it to myself
If I did that, that would make it real
That would mean that I would have to feel
I would have to cry and grieve for the little girl inside of me
I'd have to watch her die again
and relive the day her innocence ended and the lie began
To dig that up and exorcise it is great deal more than I can handle
I push that secret back in its place and put the mask back on my face
Someday I'll let her cry for me when I'm stronger
but for now I'll hold on to it a little while longer
cause what would I be without these chains
Maybe I'm afraid to be free, afraid to feel happy
It's always eluded me
If I started to enjoy it now, it wouldn't be long till some else came along
and took it away

NERVOUS

Under the concentrated gaze of your eyes
My legs feel like jelly
In my stomach awakens the flutter of butterflies
You make me shiver on the outside
and quiver on the inside
My words knotted in tongue ties
Heart beating wildly against my chest
like an animal trying to escape its prison
Wrap my arms across my tender breast
in attempt to hide the excitement that has risen
Cross my legs at the knee
Thigh kissing thigh trying to abate the heat
each time you look at me
Electricity surges from my head to my feet
Shocking my nerves
My senses heightening
The rains coming down
as images of you and me flash like lightning
If only you knew the chemical reactions
that multiplies by fractions
at the light of speed
with just the thought that we have a chance at relativity
In our equation, Ecstasy equals Me Coming 2
I can't fight the gravitational pull
The pull that has me gravitating towards you
I'm nervous when normally I can hold my cool
Fear, excitement, lust and wonder
mixed together in my body to create a fool
Embarrassment takes over and tells me to leave
If I walk away I may never again feel this high
I may never meet someone who forces me to remember how to breathe
I may forever wonder what could've happened and why
My kismet opportunity will be gone
The moment when the earth planets moon and stars aligned
So that you and I could have this moment in time
I muster up my courage, dig my heels into the earth and mentally pray
open up my mouth and out slides a barely audible, "Hi."
After hours together you reveal, "I was really nervous."
I smile and admit that I was nervous too
and so began the journey of two

I FORGIVE

If only forgiveness was like a shirt or dress
If I could simply pull it over my head and down my body
I would surely wear it all day and night
If it were so easy to forgive that I could slip into it
like a negligee or some type of lingerie,
I would gladly put it on to attire me during the darkest of nights
If only forgiveness was some amusement park ride
that I could ride to erase my fear,
I would happily stand in line and wait my turn
to ride the ride and hopefully spurn
the anger I carry deep inside
If only forgiveness was as simple as reading a book
I would linger between its pages until I felt the calm inside
that I've been seeking for ages
If only forgiveness were like the setting of the sun
I would allow it to disappear
and welcome the clemency to come
If it meant that by morning light
I would have forgotten the wrongs that were done
If only forgiveness were easy
I would give amnesty so freely
and my life would be given back to me
Even though I don't want to hurt
Every day is filled with pain
Even though I longed to forgive
Forgiveness never came
My heart hardened and my bitterness grew
I never gave up the hope that someday, somehow, someway
Maybe in my final breath on my final day
that mercy will come and take the pain away

I'M HERE FOR YOU

You've been through pain
So strong
I wish I could've stopped it
from hurting so long
Things may get worse
Life may go wrong
but always remember
whenever you feel blue
I'm always here for you
Life is about love
and I want you to know
My heart holds so much
it would like to show
So call me up
or just swing by
anytime you need to cry
I'll be your shelter against the rain
All I want is to ease your pain

A BLESSING IN DISGUISE

She knows you better than you know yourself
She shares with you pieces of herself
when she feels it's necessary
but she keeps the best parts for those she loves the best
She knows everything and admits to knowing nothing at all
She's the teacher and the student at the same time
She doesn't have a problem with the times that you fall
She cares more about the times that you don't get up
She plays the mirror, if you need to see your reflection
Other times, she'll be the voter if you need an election
She'll be your coach or your greatest cheerleader
and she somehow senses just when you need her
She's beyond anything you can believe
because she fulfills so many needs
without understanding her impact
If you are ever so lucky to have someone that respects you
when you don't even know you should be respected
yet never seems affected
then you are fortunate indeed
She's amazing to me and I'm so glad that she's able to see
and appreciate the real me.

I AM CHANGING

I am changing
Slowly breaking free
from the past transgressions that imprison me
I'm evolving
and deciding who deserves absolving
I've learned that I must change for me
so I can find inner peace
Each day is a new trial; a new chance
to advance
and see the blessings unfold

Section 3:
Reflections of a
Stranger

BLIND, BUT NOW I SEE

I was blind at one time
but now I see
I can't take credit for this vision
Time opened my eyes for me
I spent so much time focusing on everyone else
examining what they have that I don't
Wondering how they think and how they feel
I didn't care about my own thoughts
They were insignificant to the bigger picture
I wanted to be one of many,
not one alone
I wanted to blend in with the masses
and fit in among all classes
A chameleon changing my appearance
to fit every situation
The problem became that I changed so much
that I lost who I was
I had to rediscover me
I didn't even know my own likes and dislikes
I never took the time to find out
I was too busy studying others' preferences
To consider and cultivate my own
I was a tape recorder
placing my self-discovery on pause
to record and playback the desires of others
I passed every test and found myself with a Degree in invisibility.
Another faceless number in the mass of robotic comings and goings
I forgot that I was born as the only me in the nation
I better take this opportunity to get to know me
for I will never exist again
I washed off the grime of daily life with the tears of my lost soul
Slowly, I figured out who lived within
My thoughts and feelings
My spirituality
and I was surprised to discover that
She's been beckoning me

IF THE WORLD BELONGED TO ME

If the World Belonged to Me
I'll tell you what I'd
I'd plant a special tree
just for you
I'd grow it so strong and tall
that heaven would meet its leaves
You could climb it and sit among the stars
anytime you please
I'd go to you backyard
and turn the dirt to its sands
I'd take the great ocean
in the palm of my hands
When you look out the window
what a sight you will see
if the World belonged to me
But I don't own the world
and that will never be
but my heart is mine to give
and you can have it for free

THE FIRST YEAR

Great expectations and fabricated ideas of how their life would be
now has them at each other's throats
Neither understanding the other's wants
Neither communicating their needs

She says that she doesn't recognize the man she married
He used to tend to her every desire
He used to surround her with flowers
He used to tell her that he loved her every hour
He doesn't do any of it anymore

He says that she's not the woman he first met
She used to wear lingerie to bed every night
She used to like sports and watch his favorite shows
She used to cook all the time
She doesn't want to anymore

She complains that he doesn't help out enough
He complains that nothing he does is appreciated
She wants it done in her time
He wants to wait until he's ready to do it
They fight about what to do, when to do it and how

They are fighting for space
Fighting for time
Fighting for what used to be
Fighting about what it is now
In reality, they are fighting change

They are both changing into people that now have to care
They have to think about someone else
Care about what someone else thinks
They have to face criticism
They have to see themselves through someone else's eyes
All the little things they chose to ignore are now magnified
They have to realize that neither is perfect
They are slowly being pulled out of denial
They are being forced to look inside
They can no longer hide
This person gets to see the real you
and this person could help to heal you

REFLECTIONS OF A STRANGER

For ten years, I never really saw her
When I looked in the mirror
my view of her was always clouded by
an amalgamation of beliefs passed on to me
by people who never gave her a chance
They dumped their hopes and wishes
their missed opportunities and mistakes
their misgiving and misfortunes
on the mold of who she was to become
Her vision was blurred and she found herself
misguided into believing who she is isn't good enough
She looked better through their eyes
She altered her life and fought hard to fit their desires
She ignored her own needs to keep peace
She deferred her dreams to fulfill their ideas of her
until one day she looked in the mirror and didn't even know
the face staring back at her
This stranger seemed so different from me
This person was begging for my attention and love
To love her meant to go against everyone else
The fear of losing their love kept me away from the mirror
When I finally met all their expectations and still felt empty
I looked for her in the mirror
She stared back at me with vacant eyes void of hope
She'd been in the dark so long that she could barely see
She was merely a shell of her former self, barely recognizable
I neglected her for so long that she nearly died
I've set forth to nurture her back to life
I won't spend the next ten years ignoring her needs
I will build her up and back to health
until the reflection of her
mirrors the view I have of me

REMARKABLY HAPPY

I am amazingly content
Things can always be better
but I'm comfortable with where I stand now
I feel right in my skin
I smile without warning
I live in gratitude
Eternally inspired by life's small mysteries
and impressed by its mini-miracles
I am blessed by consistent heaven-sent opportunities
I can feel myself being prepared to take my throne
by passing each practice test that crosses my path
on the journey to my ultimate graduation

I'm swimming in appreciation
bathing in adoration
and abundantly rained on by hope
It washes over me in reassurance
sending me afloat in a flood of realizations
I am overjoyed to be here
to be allowed to wake each morning
to be given another chance to do something great
to touch people with my heart and words
My voice plants seeds of knowledge
that are nurtured by my actions
and eventually grow into wisdom
Imparted and well received
God's thoughts flow from my lips
as I am a vehicle of His desire and will.
He drives me to succeed
He teaches me how to believe
that I deserve good things
simply because I am me

I am deliriously excited
drunk with praise and
pregnant with potential
My life is anything that I create it
I give birth to my experience
I feed my possibilities the milk of success to satisfy my future
I burp my past releasing the exhalations that invoke pain
as they infect with swollen doubt

and expanding insecurity
I clothe my goals in robes of financial security
protecting their vulnerable naked nature
Through all these things, I shelter my happiness
and encourage it to grow.

I am remarkably happy
My smile is painting a display
Specifically designed to convey
my feelings and clearly say that happiness
has finally found its home within me

NO MORE BABY-DADDY

The time has come when we need to require more
of our men and our boys
It's not okay to walk away from the life you create
It's not okay to create life with someone other than your wife
It's not acceptable.
It's the harder road and the difficult way
Take a look and really see the destruction you contribute to
When you are only concerned about you
There are many angry young men walking these streets
killing each other over material things
They are really angry at watching their mothers struggle
and at having no father around
They internalize the lesson of disrespect
and take it out on each other and innocent men, women and children
Young girls looking for love between their legs
Loving men that don't really deserve
Never understanding their own worth
because the model of a man's love walked out of their life
The model of the man's love didn't make their mother a wife
so they would never expect a man to truly love them
They are mentally, physically abused and feeling used
but that's what they've been taught
All because their father left their mother to figure it out
It's time to stop passing the blame
and reclaim the family
The measure of a man is how he takes care of his children
What would your measure be based on that reality
The tribe needs you to survive
Your abandonment is killing the village
Take a stand
Turn around and be a man
We need you

MOTHER EARTH

Why must you be so cold?
Have I abused you for too long?
Using your resources and giving you nothing in return
Tearing up your heart and watching you burn
Mother Earth, why do you cry?
Weeping for children that watch you die
In vain, you try to wash the hurt away
In rain, you try to rebuild
only to watch your creation continually killed
Mother Earth, are you burning up with fever?
Each year we must suffer unbearable heat
Scorching earth warms your shoes and burns your feet
Making it harder to grow what we eat
Yet, we won't save you
We won't conserve
Maybe we don't deserve the beauty we chose not to preserve
Are we not your children?
Have you not given us a place to live?
Hopefully, it's not too late and you can still forgive
Maybe if we try to care and nurture you better
You won't leave us forever
Earth mother, let your tornado and hurricane winds slow
Give us time to show you that we now know
that you can live without us, but we can't live without you

LOVE BELONGS

Love is something so delicate
and so sweet
that I consider myself lucky
that you chose to give it to me
I've fought the hard fight
and lived through defeat
to find you standing next to me
being everything that I need you to be
Life is such a funny thing
You spend your time chasing a dream
only to wake up and find someone next to you
loving the you that you never knew
Doing the things that you longed to do
Pushing you to the dream that you belong to
Love together forever they offer you
without hesitation
The answer to your question
Love is loving you
Look into love's eyes
Do you see forever
because forever sees you?
A moment in time
A lifetime long
In all things you'll be fine
Like the melody of a song
I'll sing for life
and forever you will sing along.

I'M SORRY

Who knew how hard it would be
to admit that I was wrong
I was placed in charge of your life
and I assumed that meant that whatever I did had to be right
I made mistakes along the way
but it's hard for me to say
I'm sorry that I couldn't provide all that you needed
It goes beyond clothing and feeding
but it's difficult for me to express how much I care
I thought it was just enough for me to be there
I didn't realize that it was something that you wanted to hear
In order to shower you with love, I had to get past my own fear
I had to get past my own hang-ups and insecurities
I had to get past my own resentment and jealousies
I was still a child when you came into my life
I was forced to become an adult for you
It wasn't your choice and I'd never blame you
I just did what I had to do
I had to learn and grow while teaching you the things
that I still didn't know
We learned together at times
and I find that I'm still learning
I did the best that I could to make your life fulfilling
I did the best that was humanly possible considering
Now you are an adult and have far surpassed what I've accomplished
Still you are waiting for me to give you something
even though you have the ability to provide for yourself
I can't change the past and I don't know the future
but I know that you have to find a way to let it go
You keep yourself stuck in a time that you are beyond
If it's what you need to hear and will help you to move on
I will say it for you to hear
I'm sorry that I wasn't there for you in the way that you needed me to be
I'm sorry that I couldn't give you all that you needed from me
I love you more than life itself
Let go of the pain I caused unknowingly
and seize your dreams

IF I KNEW THEN...

Sometimes, I long for the days of innocence
Back when the most I was wishing for from him
was my very first kiss
When I didn't even know what came next
or the power of what was hiding beneath my dress
The simple act of holding hands sent fire through me
We talked on the phone for hours about everything
and I felt like you truly knew me
There was little to worry about beyond the time we spent together
and we were too young to begin to think about forever
There was no concern about marriage, weddings or babies
There was just you and me
It seems so long ago that the sweetest love I was to know
was in my grasp and I didn't even realize
As time went on and I grew older, I let it go
I thought that I was missing out on something better
I couldn't wait to push the limits and taste forbidden fruit
In my heart insecurity took root
as I lent my body to men that barely cared for my well-being
I searched for love in shallow feelings
I tried to mold something solid out of fluid intentions
I lost myself in pure disenchantment
Yanked from the fairytale hopes and dreams
and into the reality of boy meets girl
There is no magic in the world
for the girl that is loose with her god-given treasure
It will cost you more than a moment of pleasure
Love cannot be born of two souls losing themselves in the act
So fast to move on and to be grown
If only I had known
Now I long for the time before sex entered the equation
I wish for the magic and romance I once threw away
and I know in my heart that I will find it someday

I AM READY FOR LOVE.

In my early teens to late twenties
I looked for you under every rock
around every corner
All I found were mirages
Projections of what I thought love should be
They didn't hold up to your rules
Instead of waiting for your pure gold
I was walking around with costume jewels
I thought I could avoid hurt before it got me
I pushed him away, one after another
Dated one brother while lusting for the other
Jumped from relationship to relationship
like lily pads on still water
If real love showed up, I wouldn't know
I still taste the fear
The danger is still present and clear
Instead of suppressing it deep inside
I will share it with my love and allow it to soothe
Soft harmonies so bittersweet
I can't wait until the day we meet
I've finally gotten to know me
So I can give myself to you
The strong arms of love wrap around
while the mind tries to understand
There are times when I don't comprehend
my own actions, dimensions, and depths
but give me time
Flip the hourglass and before the sand reaches the end
I will have reinvented myself
Offering my spirit, body and mind
My energy given to seek what ye shall find
We are puzzles half-done
Pieces scattered about and mixed into one
I'll complete me and you'll complete you
then we'll come together
and we'll figure out how the puzzles fit
so that we'll be complete forever
Tell me what is enough
to prove I am ready for love

HER

There's this girl I know
She's been around all my life
and up until this time
I've tried to ignore her
I thought she was insignificant to my happiness
To me, she's pretty much a loser
that's why I would never chose her and in turn
I abuse her
while I chase after every someone else
that in my mind would represent
the love I believed I need to survive
Each time that person was proven to be the wrong one
Years I wasted trying to find the missing pieces to the puzzle
when I had it all the time
She was always mine
and with her comes the love that I dreamed of
She stares back at me with loving eyes
and quickly forgives my misdemeanor
In her, I found love
In love, I found me
She is my reflection
I love every little imperfection
I accept her for who she is
Finally, I see
The love that I've been searching for all this time
was for myself to love me

GRANDMOM

I remember her hands the most
She would work in her garden or spend the day cleaning
The afternoon baking or cooking but no matter what it was
whenever she touched me her hands were soft
They were reassuring and comforting
Her house always smelled like something sweet or something good to eat
She cooked enough food for those there and those that might show up
She was thoughtful that way
She always had something for the children
Cookies, cakes or candies
She would grease my scalp with Dixie Peach and try to braid my hair
even though her hands loss strength as she grew older
I would sit on a stool between her knees
as she combed and brushed my hair
Together we watched soap operas in the afternoon
and relished the summer breeze flowing through the screen door
I would sit in the kitchen while she baked cakes from scratch
I marveled at how she would measure ingredients from memory
with no book or recipe to follow
She knew exactly how much flour, salt and sugar.
She'd dip her finger in the batter and the taste told her what was missing
She had that same knowledge about everything else too
If I didn't feel well, she always knew exactly what would make me better
She could look in my eyes and tell if I needed a hug
or just a simple reassuring smile
I never questioned if she loved me because I could always feel it
She had no problem telling me what I needed to hear
She took me everywhere
Through her I learned how to behave when visiting company
She was always visiting a sick friend or helping the blind
She made us go to church; she cared about our spirituality
She was an amazing woman
Unfortunately, I lost her before I was old enough to really get to know her
but she's still here for me in my dreams.
Anytime, I'm troubled when I go to sleep
I know that Grandmom will be there

LOST WORLD

Borrowed money
Borrowed time
Borrowed hearts
Stolen minds
Jacked up thoughts
Recklessly polluted
Disrespectful youth
Bodies used
Futures abused
Suffering abound
Lost, but never found
Kidnapped hopes
Raped dreams
Murdered wombs
Destroyed earth
Materialism consumes
Premature birth
Satisfaction out of touch
Collapsed veins
Faith bleeds
Spilling through the streets
Gunfire explodes
Fear reloads
Solace eluding
Reasons confusing
Muffled cries
"why's" amplify
Senseless thinking
Reacting
Attacking
Same skin
Same eyes
Another person dies
Fight for survival
Freedom to be
Oppressed
Suppressed
Have we regressed?
Are we sinking?
Wilting like flowers in the garden
Deprived of nourishment

POETIC EXHIBITION

If poetry were sex
I would write all night
over and over again
My words would go deep
moving slowly and expertly
through your consciousness
They would caress your mind
while stroking your senses
Each word would join together
to create a feeling of ecstasy
to those that chose to hear
My pen would move across the page with ease
Smoothly and sensually teasing the paper with
the lightness of its touch
The paper would come alive with
words playfully move inside and in-between
the lines sending shocks of lightning
through them like nerves
Heightening the pleasure of literary stimulation
The stories I could tell
as my poetry book swells
in anticipation
and when it's over and done
the contents will spill across my pages
revealing my lover's feelings for poetry
as we birth anew

WE MET EACH NIGHT IN THE SHEETS

We met each night in the sheets
Lips parted, dancing tongue to tongue
With gentle fingers you spread me apart
and kiss my honeysuckle sweet
bringing tears to my eyes
as I feel you rise

Loving never felt so good as with you and me
Infatuation and ravenous desire mixed together
Hunger shown in tender bites
Passion proven on the headboard held by knuckles white
Legs pulled back, knees to chest
as you plunge in deep

Lips quivering from the stiffness in between
caressing the sweet lady petals
until her honey is released
Arching back to meet the grind
and suckle lovingly the milky cream
that spills from you inside me

A moment to rest and start all over again
Nipples rise like a phoenix on my chest
igniting burning desire
Massaging your potent masculinity
against my firm femininity
sending fire coursing through my veins
to the meeting spot of love's volcano

Silent explosions generate heat
and anticipation of the sensations
brewing beneath the skin
Mind blown asteroids shoot through my nerves
to my extremities
My body becomes attuned to your touch
The lightest stroke creates a spark of lightning

You have the power to inspire convulsions
My body gripped in a tug of war as the pleasure
grows and begs to be released
I writhe in ecstasy as my mind and body
greet my soul in immeasurable bliss
that begins with a kiss and ends
with both of us fast asleep
between the sheets

DÉ JÀ VU

My soul is longing
and I know there is no real way
to scratch the itch
At times, I wish I could relieve this uncomfortable feeling
but I know that it's here for a reason.
I have to seek out its healing
My purpose in life is to solve my soul's equation
to figure out what karma I'm creating
to understand what issues I'm abating
If I don't, I'm doomed to return until I get it right
I will continue to fight the same fight
until I learn what I need to know
I'll continue to suffer the same challenges
until I grow
My history won't change
I'll return as the same me with a different name
My soul won't learn unless I do the work
Stop making the same mistakes
No more excuses
Halt suffering the same abuse
Change my fate.
I can choose to believe or continue to ignore
I can realize what I've been put here for
or I can return again at life's end
to go through all of this over again and again and again

WHAT I WANT YOU TO KNOW

Little girl, you are so pretty
and you always make me smile
The love in your heart is clear and apparent
You love with reckless abandon
and no conditions
You see people as they are and accept them
Please don't lose that ever
Little girl, you find beauty in everything around you
You say what you think and tell us how you feel
You cry real tears when you are hurt
and laugh loudly when you are happy
You dream and imagine
and for you life is perfect
You dance around in your prettiest dress
and beam proudly in your Sunday's best
You are so sweet and friendly
You are accepting and welcoming
Little girl, you have a light in your eyes that shines on others
You possess immeasurable power
Please preserve it as you grow
and trust the things that in your heart you know
Life will try to tell you untruths and define you incorrectly
People will try to confuse you and deceive
Don't fall for it; trust your instincts
Define yourself and your own beliefs
Stay strong, little girl as you grow into a young lady and eventually a woman
Know in your mind and your heart
that your purpose is greater than anyone comprehends
You are apart of the earth and the land
You are apart of the circle of life
You give birth to great thoughts, ideals and people
Treasure yourself and your blessings
Little girl, you renew the world with your spirit
and your soul brings a chance to revive
Not only do you bring life but you keep it alive
Your duty is great and your tears may be heavy at times
but know that they nourish the earth and make everything clean
Little Girl, the most important thing to remember
is that you were born a Princess
and you will grow into a regal Queen

MR. BLACK PRESIDENT

I could hardly believe when I heard the truth spoken
For a minute, I was sure that someone was joking
Finally, the day that a Black Man runs for President
I always try to understand the question if the world is ready
Ready for a poised, intelligent human being running the presidency
Haven't we always been ready for such a thing?
We are not so different that we can't embrace decorum
and comprehend etiquette when it's required
Pomp and circumstance is not lost on us
nor is our cultural background
To see a black man on the political trail that represents me
I think it's finally your time
I hope to watch you shine
but in the back of my mind
present times remind me
of how prejudiced we continue to be
Just because hate is not displayed in burning crosses
People want to believe that it no longer exists
but it persists in subtle and probably more destructive ways
While I think it's past time for a black man to run this nation,
one can't deny that there is clearly still a separation
between the haves and have nots
Hidden bias crawls beneath the skin of those believed to be liberal
but hopefully, you are in the position
to change not only minds but hearts
If there is any question that racism still exists in America,
who suffers cruelly in poverty?
Look to our nation's leaders, whom do they resemble?
This is where it starts
You have my vote
and I have the audacity of hope
Hope that it's time for the world to change
Hope that God believes it too
A new nation to be born of the blood, sweat and tears
and nurtured by black hands
Over 400 years ago, we made our presence known
From that time, our potential has grown
Who could foresee such an opportunity?
Barriers will be broken and minds changed
on the inaugural day when they name you
President of these United States

NAKED

Here I stand, before you
Exposed and vulnerable
Unable to hide my imperfections
Beneath a cloak
I stand in the light
so you can get a clear view
of me opening up to you
It's cold and lonely
standing here in front of you
My ugliness is exposed for scrutiny
My insecurity on full display
There's so much that could be made better
but I procrastinate for another day
Here I stand, before you
Suffering in your silence
as you inhale my presence
and I wait for you to exhale my fears
Expecting confirmation of my negative beliefs
Fighting every urge to retreat
I'm naked, before you
Your eyes scanning every inch of my presentation
Searching your reaction for some type of indication
of what you are really thinking
Building my defense to protect myself from your disdain
Trying to fool myself into believing that I could care less
The truth is that rejection would surely cause me pain
Acceptance would be bliss
So here I stand, before you
Waiting patiently as you describe
how my nakedness makes you feel
and realizing that I have a sense of relief
It was something that I didn't expect or prepare for
It comes with finally being real
and not being able to hide anymore
I'm naked, before you
And yet, it's like I'm being myself for the first time

THE TRUTH INSIDE ME

What is truth?
Is there one immaculate truth that exists for all?
Is it undeniably the way that we are all supposed to believe?
How can my truth and your truth be the same
when neither of us see things the same way?
My perception of the events is colored by the happenings in my past
What I see and hear is affected by what I believe
When I tell you the truth, I am telling you my truth
I can't be discounted or called a liar
For my truth is the truth to me
It's based on what I think feel and see
It doesn't mean that it's the truth for you.
Your thoughts and feelings are just as important
Who am I to tell you how to be or
what to believe and how to perceive?
I cannot impose my truth on you
I can't tell you what you should believe to be true
I can share with you my beliefs
and allow you the choice to see things my way
I can try to persuade and I can attempt to sway
but I cannot force you in anyway.
I can listen and understand.
I can love you despite our differences
I can choose not to judge you
I can offer you a helping hand
I cannot condemn you in my mind
or disregard you for not agreeing
I cannot discipline you for any reason
Your belief is your own and who am I to say you are wrong
What I choose to believe
is the truth that lives inside of me

I LOVE YOU

I love you
I love you so much more than I thought was possible for me
My heart swells at the mere thought of being with you
I've never trusted anyone as much as I trust you.
I live in my love for you
I see things through your eyes
I search for your opinion on decisions that affect my life
I share things that vex me during the course of the day
I'm not afraid of public display
I want everyone to know how much I love you
You are my heart's joy
You are exactly who I've been praying for
You enhance me
You romance me
You have changed me by subtle and profound means
I want to be better to make you proud of me
I love the little things about you that others aren't privy to
I love your colloquialisms and idiosyncrasies
The things that distinguish you from everyone else
I love your thoughtful ability and your kindness
I love you for dealing with my insecurities
In your love for me you impart some blindness
You don't call me on all my mistakes and choose to let some slide
Sometimes you force me out and other times you let me hide
In every act I feel your love.
In my heart and soul I know that you care
I feel so fortunate to have the opportunity to behold such beauty
Sometimes I wonder how I could be so lucky
What did I do right to deserve someone like you?
The best part about being in love with you
is that you feel the same way too
Thank you

NOW, I REALIZE

It took me a long time to make the connection
to see what I was doing to myself in the present
was strongly connected to how I was treated in the past

Now, I realize
The transgressions I suffered as a child didn't die
instead they grew with me
like a cancer they ate away at my self-esteem
In my teenage years, I searched for the same type of pain and hurt
because I believed that was what I deserved and needed
The cancer thrived on self-punishment and
I continued to feed it

As a child, I was hurt by the ones I loved
Therefore, I learned that love equaled pain
I believed them to be one and the same
While I wished for love not to hurt
deep inside I didn't believe or trust it unless it made me cry
I couldn't put my faith in it unless I questioned it.
Love had to prove itself to me for me to imbibe
so I tested it relentlessly

If it left me I felt disappointed but I proved myself right
I thought in order to have love in my life that love had to survive the fight
What I didn't understand was that love could never win
It would never get through my defense
I went through my twenties wondering why I kept meeting people
that continued to deprive me and make love difficult
The truth is that I brought them into my life
because I knew they would never love me
and proved my thoughts and beliefs
Giving me a sick sense of relief
that I wouldn't have to be vulnerable and let someone in

Now, I realize
I can do better now that I know
Love doesn't have to hurt and I want it in my life
I'm ready to open up and trust love to love me right
It's not going to happen overnight,
but now instead of battling love I'm behind love in the fight.
Happiness is something that I deserve and I know that now

What happened in the past will stay there and is no longer in my reflection
I've gone through the examination and dissection
I'm killing the cancer of pain with every step I take
I no longer hurt myself for someone else's mistake
Now, I realize
That true love is my fate

PHILADELPHIA BLUES

Clouds weep on city streets
of the City once known for Brotherly Love
rains down from above
to lovingly wash away signs of descent
Bullet casings lay
on the ground where children play
mid-day
and where lost souls
suck away their life on a pipe
in the middle of the night
Hollow eyes stare down the barrel
smoke rises
as life bleeds on the concrete
No remorse
Someone's brotherly love
future halted
instead of exalted
for positive contribution
Your mirror self dies
because he is you and you are he
a little piece of you suffers demise
when you take another life

Sun rises on city streets
of the City known as Brotherly Love
chase away the shadows of night
embrace the right to life
nurture the children and make them grow
The fear of death will not stop us
The possibility of what will be
is inviting
One day it will be uniting
but we will keep on fighting
Each sun promises a chance to do better
The rainbow comes after the storm
but it must rain down strong
to clean the streets
of Philadelphia blues

ATTENTION SEEKER

Attention seeker
local House speaker
searching for the spotlight by inviting events into your life
Headlining the latest tragedy
Reporting the personally engineered drama in your disastrous storyline
Every day at noon is story-time
Tall tales and fables alike
Robotic-like as you deliver the daily script of Man against himself
the constant fight of you against life
Like a billboard, your struggle is on display
and dramatically, you describe your plight
as if your struggles are the multiplied equation of those around you
Your cross to bear is so much heavier than others
If you used your gift of sight, you would see the reality
that those who listen and pretend to care
expect to be bombarded with your unconscious desire for fame
that you think you can only get by placing blame

Attention stealer
Drama is your middle name
Excuses, stories and lies seem realer
as you search for just the right thing to gain
the sympathy you desperately desire
however, the audience gives you mercy instead
People that care would call you a liar
It sounds painful, but more pain is derived
in descending into easily identified lies
The cost of attention is a hefty price
You can get so caught up in your version of life
that you begin to believe the falsehoods to be truth
and can't tell the difference any longer

Attention needy
You have a true opportunity
understand that you don't need attention from me
The attention you desire lies deep inside
once you discover it, you'll never again feel denied

OBSERVER

From the outside looking in
I watch your movements
and listen to your words
So many things reveal your thinking
Your actions dictate your insecurities
You try to mask your inconsistencies
but they peek through inevitably
Hidden behind the tough exterior
vulnerability is cowering in fear
The louder you scream to threaten others
certainty increases defeating deception
and unearths your panic
You are fooling only yourself
When you attempt to keep others away
They are always present and seeing everything
They echo your needs
whether it's what you think you want or seek to avoid
Observers are watching your moves
Your thoughts spill in the silence between your words
and the space between your steps
What you think about yourself is evident
What you think about others is based on how you feel about yourself
Your reaction is a reaction to what you don't appreciate in your own actions
While you believe you are hiding what you don't want others to know
You are really telling them truths instead of lies
The response you receive is obscured by your beliefs
Observers are seeing more than you think
They see honestly more than they are deceived
If you are truly lucky you'll find one
that won't allow you to get away trying to camouflage
who will tell you that it's a mirage
and rescue you from your delusion

WAKE UP!

Sometimes, life boggles my mind
It makes no sense to be in a constant state of why
You're born, you learn, you live and you die
In between you make so many mistakes
You survive gunshots and earthquakes,
a tsunami, starvation, racism and war,
and at the same time you have to figure out what you were put here for
Born with a purpose unforeseen
Living your life in order to realize your dream
Birthed into adversity
Skin color decides your ride in life
but every color of skin deals with some type of strife
Who puts us through it?
We do it to each other
The one that you call sister; the one that you call brother
The more you love them, the more you put them through
Love gives life to hate
This can't all be fate
People are trying to win
but someone has to be the loser
People trying to use
and still avoid feeling like a user
People trying to play
without ever being played
People trying to save
but never be saved.
Taking turns playing the victim and the victor
At times, being the predator
and not acknowledge the prey
Going through the same cycle day after day
Crops grow, cocks crow, and the sun will rise and shine
but we create the ties that bind
The hands of the clock continue to turn the time
and we continue to create misery in the mind
Things will never change
until we accept the blame
for the state we have created
If not, you'll keep moving through life sedated
WAKE UP!

POWER OF THE MIND

There was a time
When I believed that anything worth having was worth fighting for
I don't think that way no more
Anything worth having is worth earning
It doesn't involve a fight or a struggle
It involves being earnest
It means believing that I'm deserving

There was a time
When I thought love had to hurt to work
I thought it required great sacrifice
I thought that when a man treated you beneath your worth
that it didn't mean that he didn't love you, but to keep pursuit
Now, I have completely changed my mind
A man that loves you will demand your time
He will love everything about you and celebrate who you are
He will be everything you need and more
Love is not something you earn
It's something you're given because you believe you deserve

There was a time
When I thought struggle made sense
I assumed that it was my road to travel
The journey of life will be difficult at times, but we create the struggle
Roadblocks don't exist
Ceilings are illusions
There is nothing holding you back, but you
There's no cap to what you can do
Potential is exponential

There was a time
When I believed what I was told, but now I know the truth
Who I am is who I believe
What I believe is me
I chose to believe in positivity
Who I am is happy
Happy is my new reality
It bends and shapes to my beliefs
I am me

WITH THESE WINGS

With these newfound wings I fly
The sky has opened up for me
with these newfound wings I glide
I ride along the nighttime breeze
Places that I once refused to go are no longer a mystery
For I have opened up my eyes
and I can see what stands in front of me
Wings of gossamer and angel dust
for logical reasons, shouldn't hold me up
but they caress and embrace the wind
and I ascend to the sky moving among the clouds
brushing against the trees, touching their leaves
What makes these wings defy gravity's laws?
They are supported by the strength of faith
I am soaring on the power of my belief
I believe that I can fly and therefore, I can
Illusions no longer oppress my mind
forcing me to think small and limit my abilities
I've embraced my greatness and now understand
that the obstacles that I once thought prevented me
were created by me and cease to exist
 Mentally, I have stepped out of my own path
and I'm ready to see myself proceed
These wings are the creation of inner guidance
and my inner desire to succeed
Any obstacle I perceive, I simply expand my wings
and fly above any type of negativity
to sail in the light of love
Positive reinforcements come to support me
as I continue to elevate my thinking
My destiny is waiting with open arms
The Universe provides me with all my needs
and when I've reached the plateau where my crown resides
I will pass down my wings to a Prince or Princess
that needs to understand their ability
to be the next King or Queen
and live one's own dreams

WHO AM I TO BE BRILLIANT, GORGEOUS, TALENTED AND FAMOUS?

Who am I to be brilliant, gorgeous, talented and famous?
Who am I not to be?
I was put on the earth to live
I was given the gifts to give
I'm fortunate to have and receive love and so lucky to recognize it
For so long, I was so lost in
what I never got that I thought I should
or what I thought I needed to be better
that I misunderstood the gift I'd already been given
The gifts I received at birth
and cultivated as I grew into me
God put me on this earth for a purpose
In this life, there are seasons
Some life begins in spring and ends in the winter
but I am fortunate to be here all year
Why would I squander such a blessing and waste each passing day
when someone won't be here to see tomorrow
Life is a blessing and not worth forgetting
Each day is an opportunity to try something different
and be better than you were the day before
Arguments, mistakes and embarrassments appear smaller
in your rearview as you continue forward in the journey
of who you are meant to be
So why not live with reckless abandon?
Don't be afraid to laugh loudly and to smile for no reason
Be a hundred percent of you and allow others the same
There is only one of me and if I am not me then who will ever be?
Who am I to be brilliant, gorgeous, talented and famous?
Who am I not to be?
It's my God-given right
I can only shine with my God-given light
It's how I wake up in the morning and how I go to bed at night
It's my reason for being and what keeps me believing
Hopefully, you will see yourself in me
and live to your highest ability

www.ingramcontent.com/pod-product-compliance
Lightning Source LLC
LaVergne TN
LVHW091203080426
835509LV00006B/815